SShh..

Trauma doesn't only create things..it takes them away..

By

J C Lindsay

ISBN: 978-1-917425-15-5

Dedications

As always to Uri. I love you. You are absolutely everything to me and the sole reason I exist . I am so proud of you, the person you are and are still becoming.

I also would like to dedicate this to the most beautiful, and genuine soul that I've ever come across... Mr Jonny Daniels. You will never realise the hole in which you pulled me out of. Just seeing your strength, openness and generosity, truly amazes me.

To Dan whose wise words gave me that lightbulb moment of truth right when I need to hear it and to start putting them thoughts into action.

For the people and the conversations, we have had with one another where we opened our hearts... you know who you are.

And of course, to all of you who have never been able to live because you have been too busy just surviving.

Foreword

An intimate look at the struggles that sexual abuse most certainly leaves you with as you navigate your way through this thing we call life.

The chapters that follow are all short and sweet, purposely done that way. The same way we're expected to handle sexual abuse, which in turn reveals itself as a lifetime of trauma, as survivors were expected to accept it, deal with it already and quickly move on as it presents itself as a very uncomfortable situation for everyone around us for many different reasons.

How on earth do you think it feels for us? Except for any of us that do know. knows unfortunately it doesn't work like that.

If only it did, then maybe we wouldn't find ourselves here, trying to connect with someone or something that resonates with us, and the weirdness our personalities take on while trying to find that something, our own little safe space, coping space, where we can breathe out, if only for a short time.

Chapter 1

Flags and bunting

It was a lovely bright day, clear blue skies, warm and sunny. You could feel the excitement surrounding this special occasion.

It was 29 July 1981. Everyone had joined in on this fairytale story, the wedding of Prince Charles and Lady Diana. I was only six at the time and the whole community had come together and we were having a street party! We were lucky; we had a really large oval grass island in between, separating each side of the road from the other, but of which could bring us all together when needed to share in this magic moment. People brought out their tables and chairs and pushed them all together; bunting was draped everywhere and little plastic flags were being waved frantically by all the kids running up and down the grass. Everywhere you looked was a sea of red, white and blue! As happy as a day like this was supposed to be, my nightmare was already in full swing.

I ran across back to my house as I was bursting to use the toilet. I was in such a rush to pee I never thought to slide the little lock across the bathroom door. And there I found myself again… trapped! He must've been watching the whole time, seeing me come back to the house. It was definitely a good day for him, for the sickness he carried in his mind. He had me exactly where he wanted me: on my own, straightaway pushing the door open, asking if I was okay and if I needed any help, quickly thinking ahead and snatching the roll of tissue out of my reach, so he knew he would be doing it.

All of this had been going on for a few years by then. As strange as it might seem, the actual touching didn't seem to bother me. In that moment all I could think about was getting caught and that it was me that had been doing something wrong! As usual, my hand was grabbed and rubbed across his trousers, his crotch. Just at that moment, the back door slammed, which meant someone else was here.

Thank God. He quickly positioned himself on the other side of the door, like he was just waiting to use the bathroom – how clever, eh..

I could hear my brother's voice, asking what he was doing, to which he replied, "Just waiting for the loo." I could make my getaway while my brother was there, and get back to the celebrations like nothing had ever happened – but it had, and had been since I was around three years old.

Chapter 2

Thrown to the wolves

They were four of us, five including my mum: two boys and two girls, and I was the youngest. My mum was a single mum; not a separated mum whose ex still had the kids at the weekend, but a single mum who is single because she does absolutely everything on her own, physically, mentally and financially. We didn't have much in the way of material things, but then who did back then? It was a different time, such a time when we didn't need things, not like we "think" we need today in this very much materialistic world which we unfortunately find ourselves in.

She was a great mum; she always provided for us, took little jobs in between school times so she could provide us with a roof over our heads and food in our bellies! It must have been so hard for her. As I've gotten older and become a parent myself I've only just realised, especially as she too was dealing with a lot of other unseen things. It was just a normal household apart from this horrendous thing, which had become normalised, but I was aware I had to keep hidden. But the fact that I was hiding it just showed that in no way, shape or form was it normal! It's strange, isn't it? As little as I was, as young as I was, I was already aware and understood the trouble that this would cause within the family; maybe it's like this for a lot of us and that's why it happens so much within the family circle, and that's why the abusers get away with it: because there's that pull with the family connection.

My earliest memory of something not being right was
when I was around three. I'll tell you how tiny I was,
because I could hide under a small nest of tables, which my
mum had at the back of our living room. I'd hide from him
while he was trying to coax me out, push myself to the back
as far as I could go, try to get out of his reach, inwardly
hoping that someone, anyone, would just arrive precisely in
that very moment to save me. And at some point someone
must have, because he gave up and left me to it. But then
all I remember is being surrounded in the hallway by my
mum, nan and dad, which was unusual seeing as he was
barely ever around! He had never really been a part of my
life. My mum and him had never been together properly,
him not wanting to or being able to step up. They all seemed
to collectively ask me, "Has Uncle Lionel been funny with
you or tried to touch you?" So looking back what made
them even ask me that? I spoke to my mum about it some
forty-three years later and she had no recollection of it, but
something must've been seen or spoken about to have even
asked me, so they must have been aware of something. And
as I discuss further on in the book, that was my chance to
say something, and I didn't. I can feel now exactly the way
I felt then, in that moment when I was asked. I felt as though
I was the one going to be in bother , so I stayed silent.

Chapter 3

Jaws

I'd remembered this so clearly in my mind, the nest of tables, because it was Christmas and that's where the tree stood. Every year on Boxing Day we would go to my auntie's house for a finger buffet. I also can't remember not ever wanting to go (that's given me food for thought!) I'd been nagging my mum for ages, or rather dropping hints that I'd like the Jaws game – you know, the one where you have to collect all the pieces out of its jaws before they snap shut on you! And I was over the moon because Santa had brought me it. I can't even remember the moment when I stopped believing in Santa, or maybe.. that's because I haven't! Growing up with just my nan, had made my mum and auntie really close. Perhaps even more protective, because not too long before my aunt had,had a heart attack though she never gave in and continued to work. and it was a physical job she used to do too. She didn't really have a choice because her husband,my abuser barely gave her anything towards the upkeep of running a household! Although there was always money for his drink which was most nights, but nothing extra where the real help was needed. He always worked full-time and it seemed that everyone adored him at work; he received countless certificates and employee of the month awards – if only they knew, eh. That old saying of "what goes on behind closed doors" springs to mind. My auntie was a really good wife too, you know, where tea is on the table at a certain time after a hard day's graft, clothes washed and pressed, always making sure he was taken care of and his needs were being met.

So we were at their house, all sat around playing different games, and I go up to use the bathroom, his eyes always on me, watching, so of course when I came out of the bathroom he was there waiting to give me a piggyback down the stairs, where conveniently his hands and fingers were placed and inserted where they shouldn't have been. This continued for a few years, probably until it became too noticeable because I was getting way too old for piggybacks! Because of my age, I was mostly always with my mum if we just used nipped out to see my auntie.

My auntie and Uncle lived on the street above ours, so my brothers and sister were okay to stay at home on their own as they were eleven, fourteen and sixteen. I think even then I was aware that I couldn't say that I didn't want to go because then it would've raised the question of why not. Why didn't I want to go? Although as time has gone by and I've had a short window space to discuss it with my mum, it seemed to be known within the family; not necessarily what was happening to me but certainly not from the want of him trying! I don't know if this knowledge stretched outside of the family to his friends, his drinking buddies, that he was indeed that way inclined, but even so, nothing was ever said or done about it. Maybe it had been prevented in certain scenarios where they knew he had tried, but in no way was this going to put a permanent end to his sick behaviour.

Chapter 4

Feels like I've been thrown under the bus

As time has gone on, all these years of struggling, half of a lifetime has gone by, gone because of him and the crippling anxiety and long-term trauma I've been left with. It's not just the things it's leaves you with, but also the things it takes away from you. I totally understand the bond between family; perhaps knowing something or speaking about it could destroy a person, whether it's the person doing the abusing or a sister you love so dearly. No one could foresee the damage that would be done and the lasting effect it would have on me, would it have been an embarrassment if people knew what was going on? and then fingers would be pointed if it was all to have been brought out into the open?

Perhaps a sense of shame? Should I feel more ashamed because I didn't speak up..did I? So many questions.

Would it have been a different outcome if they definitely knew to what extent it was happening? To me now, especially as a parent, just knowing the intent would have been enough. And no matter what, that behaviour is totally wrong and we shouldn't be shielding someone just because they're family. "Blood is thicker than water" – yes, it is, so therefore a situation shouldn't be taken advantage of just because you have the means, and you shouldn't expect it to be overlooked because of the bloodline. No. Knowing what it is still like today with the abuse of woman and men, sexual violence and rape, with the main factor being whether you will be believed, it's still very hard, so how hard would it have been then? But I just wish we could've tried and somebody would have stepped up and done something – me included – where I could've felt that I was in an environment where I could have done that, and I wouldn't be here having felt the need to write this book and you wouldn't be here needing to read it! It could have been a totally different story! By doing so all we did was enable him, helped him to continue. Of course I wouldn't want to hurt my family and especially my auntie. I loved her, but that still doesn't stop me from feeling like I was thrown to the wolves to protect her. I don't have any resentment or ill feeling towards her. She had it really hard and she suffered immensely with the illness she had towards the end, and I wouldn't have wanted to hurt her even more by making her aware.

Besides, the feeling I got from everyone else was never to mention it, because of the heart attack, which, as my mum stated a long time after, " Would have killed her off had she known", whether that being physically or mentally, so I think that was the notion instilled in all of us. It's a really hard one to explain, its like the elephant in the room, we're all aware of something ,but are conscious that we cant mention it. But without wanting to sound selfish, that didn't help me, and by no means to say it in a hurtful way , but it does sometimes feel like I was thrown under the bus to protect her.

Chapter 5

Why did you give him the opportunity?

Even though we were all keeping quiet, I can never understand why he was given "extra" opportunity. Knowing now people were aware of "something" and kept it a secret without ever discussing it. Bizarre how we go along with things and just get on with it. I recall being taken on a day trip with both my auntie and uncle. When we returned home, he had me spread out on the bed, holding on to a stuffed monkey they'd just bought me on our day out! All the while my auntie was just downstairs! Did my mum think because my auntie was there that nothing would happen? Or that it would bring unwanted attention if she had said I couldn't go? The fact is I had been allowed to go with him even when I was on my own. Which I struggle to even imagine, why would I have even been allowed to go?

Apparently there was a time when he had tried to force himself on me and my brother had needed to physically pull him off me. Many years later my mum remarked that " I should be thankful that he did! "For something that should have most definitely been done anyway!

He was a drinker, he was a navy man back in the day, and they're known to like a dram, a dram of rum. He was out most nights after he'd done a full day's work, just to be social, mind; he didn't drink to get totally abbreviated as some people find it necessary to do, nor was he ever violent as again some people can be. Sundays he would go to the local cricket club and meet up with his friends. I've often wondered if they knew about his "tendencies". I remember some conversation where he'd asked my mum if it would be okay to take me with him at the weekend, I don't remember anything in particular being said, but it can't have been because there I was being allowed to go with him!

At the back of the cricket club there was an industrial site, awhere they used to store shipping containers, hundreds of them all stacked up there. It was a shorter way to cut through to the cricket ground. Many of the older containers which were worn out were scattered about unlocked or simply just rusting away. On our way going was fine, but then we had to come back.

I knew what was coming when he said, "Ooh, let's just take a look in there." I still walked in like I didn't know what was going to happen... I carried on walking to the far end knowing I couldn't be going much further as it was the end of the corrugated walls. Then as usual, the stench of his bad breath mixed with alcohol, tainted with the smell of Brut - all, warm as it engulfed my face Then grabbing my hand and putting it inside his zip which was conveniently already open. Then he'd check as we came out to make sure no one was around to have seen.

I wonder what used to run through his mind when he had these opportunities. Did he plan it or just take the chance at that precise moment in time?

Chapter 6

Parsnips and Carrots

The episode in the container was just a regular experience for me, just that it always happened someplace else, which most usually took place in the kitchen of their house, which really when you think about it was a really big risk – this sick behaviour was already risky, which he took at every opportunity, but the fact the kitchen had two doors, one leading into the dining room and the other directly into the hall, which then led straight into the living room. So while my mum and auntie were in there having a cuppa and busy talking, he was waiting eagerly with his zip down in the kitchen – where he would have had to keep both eyes on both doors in case someone came in!

They had an old dog called Duke He was a lovely, soft fluffy old thing. In the summer he used to wait for the ice cream van to come around because he was always treated to one and would always devour it! He also loved to crunch on carrots and parsnips. He would go into the larder and help himself. That was usually the way I was persuaded to leave the room: "Go with Duke and let him get a carrot." It was mainly him suggesting it and then he'd be ready and waiting; same old routine. Hot stinking breath, tinged with the Brut he'd most likely just sprayed, this time forcing his tongue in my mouth as he was fiddling around for my hand. Just the thought of it makes me feel physically sick.

There were always plenty of board games and toys to play with, And my uncle was always happy to play a game, he would suggest perhaps doing a jigsaw, which meant we had to sit at the dining room table where he had easy access and could easily sneak his hands between my legs, so blatant to do, even when there were other people around the table. Perhaps we'd be eating a meal. He knew he could do it and get away with it and that's exactly what he did. Maybe he got a kick out of it knowing he could do as he pleased. Writing these words now, remembering being sat around that table, I wish I would have had the confidence and strength to stand up in front of everyone and shout out for him to stop touching me where he shouldn't be.

Chapter 7

Nearly caught

You know sometimes I occasionally catch myself thinking, wondering if my auntie ever knew or suspected something, but hand on heart I don't think that she had any inclination of what was going on. Your mind can easily run away with you, wondering if he's doing this to me what else could he be capable of? What was their relationship like? Was he unkind to her, or did he force her to go along with something she didn't want to? But just as quickly as those thoughts come into my head, I try to bat them right back out again.

Their house had two large gardens, front and back, and which continued down the side of the house. The back was huge. I can remember picking peapods there, popping them out and eating them as we went along. They also had two outhouses, which were absolutely stifling in the summer. You couldn't hardly take the dry air in. All the normal clutter was kept in there: garden stuff, DIY stuff and old half-used paint cans. I don't even remember how I found myself in there on this occasion, but all I'll say is that it wasn't a very nice situation and as I was getting that bit older, the type of abuse seemed also to advance. Was it the fact that I was becoming a young woman, so my body was changing, or simply because he was running out of time? I was growing up.

All of a sudden, my auntie was at the door, calling out, trying to push it open! But always conscious of the situation, he had propped up an old sun lounger against it, giving himself ample time to put himself away using the excuse the lounger must have dropped from behind the door.

I can feel the heat now, the dryness in the air tightening my throat, the hot gut feeling rising up from my tummy, right the way up, filling my cheeks full of redness where I could feel them burning as she glared at me, my mind racing. What words were going to come out of her mouth?

But nothing did; the way she was just looking at me said it all: "What are you doing in here?" Straightaway, again it's you that feels like you're the one doing wrong! That I shouldn't be doing it – but what choice did I have? It was all hushed up for her sake! That dirty sense of shame washing all over me, making me think it was my fault I make him do these things he does to me. I can still feel that awkwardness that followed, just sat there, waiting. Waiting for something, but for what? There was no way I was the only one feeling it, surely.

Chapter 8

The day it all stopped

My nephew was born when I was nine and I absolutely loved him to pieces. He was such a happy little baby turning into just as happy a little boy! I spent a lot of time at my sisters with them. He was like a little brother to me, which was nice because being the youngest I never got the experience of a younger sibling. The way he used to laugh his little head off as we would sing "Noodle Doodle" as the aeroplane delivered food into his mouth!

It was around this time that I first really began to feel stressed in certain situations, which now know to be extreme anxiety. I'd always been a very shy child and would hide behind my mum's skirt when anyone came to visit, but it was always put down to shyness. Then for no reason whatsoever, or so I thought, I began struggling when it came to PE at school, getting dressed and undressed. I'd make all the excuses I could think of so I didn't have to take part. You see it's all these little things that creep in. You can't explain because you don't even understand it yourself.

Only now at forty-nine am I beginning to understand how all these things played out. Because I was so quiet it was hard to make friends, I felt different and knew it. The fact that I wasn't very outgoing made it more difficult, but I wasn't bothered. I wasn't interested going places, but for a good reason which I'll explain later.

When I look back now at my behaviour and when I started noticing it, or really I should say "feeling" it. I had a nervous feeling going out shopping with my sister. My tummy felt like it had a giant ball of rubber bands in it, gripping tighter and tighter. I felt like I was too scared to engage. Even just paying at the checkout was a problem, which was where I used to get so stressed and inwardly panic like mad! Probably on a few too many occasions, as I'm sure was to my sister's annoyance! But I was just trying to keep it together.

We used to take walks in the summer when the weather was nice and occasionally this meant calling at my auntie's so she could see how my nephew was coming along. He was just coming up to two when I had just gone eleven and he was doing that wobbly little toddler walk all around the garden, us watching carefully as there were lots of rose trees, my auntie's favourite. My uncle sent me in to get a toy gun game, which fired ping pong balls at little cardboard targets. I had to pull up the chair because I knew it was on top of the dresser in the dining room. As I reached up, I felt his hand immediately go up my dress and in between my legs. Then, just out of nowhere without even having time to think, I slapped him right across his face and blurted out, "Don't you ever, ever touch me like that again or else I'm going to tell my mum and the police." He took his hand away straightaway. I got down, put the chair back, went back out into the garden and set the targets up, still not daring to breathe, to take in what I'd just done! My face must've been showing something for my sister to ask if everything was okay.

I played that game like nothing had even happened, but it had. After all that time, it was done, just like that, it was over. I remember walking away and the largest amount of relief sighed out of me.

Chapter 9

Too busy surviving

It had stopped that day; I had made it stop.

I can't remember ever going back there, only once years later when my auntie was poorly, and as I walked past the end of her street, I wanted so much to go and see her because I knew she was still poorly. Even though she was now recovering, she still had a long way to go, but I continued walking until that voice, someone's whisper in my head, told me to turn around and go back. I'm so glad I did because she passed away shortly after and I was so grateful I'd had the chance to see her one last time.

I was around nineteen or twenty then and was kind of in my first relationship; well, if you could call it that. You know when they like it to look a certain way like it's just casual to them and everyone else, but when they're wanting something from you, all of a sudden then, they don't mind calling it a relationship! Oh what fools we can be! I occasionally went in to the local pub but because I've never been interested in drinking alcohol and the aggro that can sometimes go hand in hand with it, I preferred to stay away; besides, just not really ever liking the taste of anything and it always seems such a waste of money to me. For someone like me, like us who overthink, we need to be able to be present even more so in a particular moment .In certain situations especially when you're out ,we try our best to control what's around us. But it wasn't just that, was it?

On the times I was out I'd see my uncle arrive for last orders having made his way from the "cricket club" where he would always try to catch my attention with the offer of a drink. There was no need to get my attention; I knew exactly where he was but never once allowed my eyes to meet with his across that bar. He disgusted me. It was at that point where the guy I was seeing noticed me avoiding him. I had to be honest and I told him what he was and what he had done. I've always been so open and ready to let it all out but had never been given the chance.

I've never wanted to play the victim; more the fact, but I've always felt, and often still do the need to explain why I am the way I am ,to explain away some of those silly little behaviours which I've accumulated over the years as a coping mechanism. Even in that moment I don't think the guy knew how to handle it, that information.

What to say? What do you say?

There were times when I'd reached out to teachers when I was at upper school, but nothing ever came of it. Looking back, surely you would have at least had my mum in school to see what the hell was going on at home because her daughter was visibly struggling, but nothing. Especially since I'd also started skipping school at this point. It's like pouring your heart out writing something on the back of a leaf and that leaf just blows away down the street, never to be found or mentioned again.

It hurts to think over the years that some members of my family could easily throw out remarks about my weirdness, my reluctance or nervousness to go out, but unfortunately it's become apparent it's not with that same easiness , to ask why, and to maybe try and help me, knowing I was obviously struggling, instead of just brushing it under the carpet which seems to be the way these things are handled, only then, by leaving them unhandled can only lead one way. To devastation.

All of those missed chances for someone, anyone, to step in – but absolutely nothing. Nada. I was just trying to grasp at something ,anything, I still tend to do that now. Reaching out but there was never anyone's hand to grab, in the way

I needed or even a foot up. That's what it was like and not just for me either. When people say it was a different time, it really was, and honestly , I don't know how much and if things have gotten better. I appreciate it was a time where mindsets and behaviour were very much different, but just because somethings a certain way, doesn't necessarily make it right. We evolve in so many different ways but not in others. We really need to be better and do better. Let you're hand be the hand that someone reaches out for.

Chapter 10

I'm just not good enough

For anyone who has been sexually abused there's not a single thing in your life that it won't have touched. As a friend of mine once said, "It's absolutely xxxx It affects absolutely everything that you do."

Your mind, your body, your relationships, romantic or otherwise, your work, your friends, your family. Everyday life is one constant struggle.

You overthink, panic, indulge, over-indulge; your thought process can become an absolute living hell! You're living in survival mode 24/7.

No doubt at some point depression kicks in so you already feel different, cut off, isolated, and you know you're in trouble when you can't even summon the power to fill the washing machine or change your jim-jams, and when you start to question yourself why you're even here you're well and truly done for, engulfed in that thick cloud of fog.

I'd had a handful of relationships which had never worked . A person who has fallen or been at their lowest as opposed to someone who hasn't will tend to have a different way of looking at things, have a different understanding, and we tend to go the extra mile to make sure that others don't ever feel the same way that we have, because we know how bad things can get. Things can be misinterpreted; they take our kindness for weakness and take advantage of our loving nature and unfortunately there are many people who are like this. The absolute worst thing, the lowest thing that someone can do, is use that exact same thing that has destroyed you or is destroying you. To manipulate a situation to their advantage, to do this to another human being is to be morally bankrupt. People just continue to destroy one another. Which only makes it that much harder for us. We're trying to connect to something we think could be a normal way of going about things for us, perhaps to think we have found someone, found a connection, maybe someone who can protect us, stand up for us, and when it doesn't work out, leaving us feeling there is something wrong with us and that we really are worthless, we always have been, because were looking for something, most of the time not knowing what that something is, we plough everything we've got into a relationship and it's just not reciprocated on a level that we need, if on any level at all. Then the feeling of being used for whatever reason only intensifies. When that something we've been , searching for, is already inside us and always has been, just waiting for us, while we were searching for it elsewhere, its been waiting for us all along, for you to acknowledge it and then were able to start the heal ing process, we need to look for ourselves, not for anyone or anything else.

Because we have a different way of having to manage things, we develop coping mechanisms. It can be hard to make friendships and especially maintain them. Even family who are closest and you feel a certain comfortableness with, there's always an element of distance you have to keep, and because of the way you are you can't join in on the most normal of celebrations like birthdays and Christmas etc, but isn't that precisely what life's meant to be about? That human connection. I honestly don't know what it's like to actually live life, because I've always been on high alert. It's never ending. You're too busy panicking to be in the moment, when you should be able to just enjoy something, anything. Even if its just for a short while.

Chapter 11

What's wrong with me

Let's be honest here: we are damaged. We're bound to be after what we've been through, there's no getting away from that, and we will never be able to fully ever break away from it, so all we can do is just try to manage it the best we can. We are VICTIMS but were also ones who have SURVIVED and now we NEED to CONQUER whatever is holding us back from living the best life we can and also deserve..

I'd always struggled and gone through many depressive periods, but in between I'd always managed to hold down a job, as hard as it was, especially after having my son and raising him on my own, I had no choice, I had to work to provide for us, for him. But as I was getting older and each time I felt my depression coming on, it seemed to be a hell of a lot worse than the previous time! I just didn't know how much more of this I could actually take. Was it ever going to end? I was a nervous wreck.

The actual work I could manage it was the journey there and back that seemed to cause me the most distress, going out amongst the bustle of life.

When I wasn't at work I was more or less always at home, in the place where I felt safe. It just seemed to be when I was going out, that horrendous build before having to leave the house. But for the last few years even that too had become overpowering, feeling that sense of dread while I was in my home, inside flushes of excruciating horribleness that waved over me, apparently for just no reason. That was the only place where I had always felt safe.

My GP had always been very supportive of me and after many years of being on medication, she referred me to a counsellor who specialized in trauma and PTSD. I had to wait a good while but at least I knew it was coming, something was on the horizon, and all I had in my mind is that I'm going to be able to get this sorted once and for all. All I wanted was to just let it all out. It was bursting at the seams to be released and had and still does present itself through tears. I'm surprised my tear ducts haven't totally gone out of action from overload!

I just needed them to tell me what was wrong with me. Why was I so messed up? Couldn't even nip out to the shop for pint of milk without agonising over it for five hours the night before, knowing we'd run out! Honestly its no joke, when normal people don't even give it a second thought as they rush out the door and go about their business. We had twelve sessions. I'm so open and emotionally available, the conversation just flows out of me like a river; after all, it had built up for forty-odd years! I couldn't get my words out quick enough! At last, someone who was just there to listen to me while I got it all out. It was good just to have that release each week. There were two things, important things, I came away from those sessions with, one of them being the most important question I needed an answer to: "Why was my anxiety so bad that I could barely leave the house?" And he explained and it just seemed so simple. The reason being each time the sexual abuse happened was out of the house. It always took place somewhere else. So as my little brain tried its best to process it, it tried to protect itself by telling it that's when the bad things happen, whilst I was out! And as easy as that, my question had been answered and I could see the reason why it would actually make sense and cause that trigger. I was so grateful and still am because that simple answer explained away all those years for me, so thankyou Paul. It was like a weight had been lifted off me. Because it had never been acknowledged or validated, it didn't seem worthy, I didn't feel worthy of anything, and so there it was: my explanation, my reason. I'd had one all along that was valid.

Chapter 12

Ten words: the day it all came together

The second thing I came away with from that trauma counselling wasn't as good as the first, but still very much just as important. It was, why am I still feeling the same way? But knowing and doing are two different things entirely. They tell you where you need to be and perhaps should be, but not how to get there. Now this was a further two years down the line from that original counselling and I still wasn't able to move forward and was feeling at my absolute worst, especially as I felt a failure because it hadn't worked, I hadn't got better. I used to blame myself further by thinking the professionals know what they're doing, so why am I just not getting it? Am I that stupid?

Then one day as I was scrolling through my Instagram as you do, an advertisement popped up. One sentence, ten words. Those ten words were "YOU CANNOT THINK YOUR WAY OUT OF A FEELING PROBLEM".

Wow… in that moment and now each time I read those words, I get that sense of clarity as I did the very first time seeing them. They meant the world to me and still do, making sense like nothing else ever had. It felt like a full circle moment. It's taken a minute to get here.

Since that first real therapy experience I had, I really wasn't in a good place, and by that I mean I was really struggling to the point of actually not wanting to be here anymore. I couldn't see a way out of this absolutely brutal place. I just couldn't take the way in which my mind overthinks and has to analyse every single thing no matter what it might be. The excruciating gut wrench I feel each time I have to leave the house, but when I stumbled across those ten words – everything just seemed to click, I understood perfectly, those words were referring to me. My mind saying one thing and my body feeling something else, I held that pain in my body. And because I'd always felt like a fraud and that people looked at me in that way. When I say I stumbled onto this book, I truly believe nothing is a coincidence and everything happens for a reason, good or bad. I was meant to see them words, to read that book, someone had put them in my way.

They had actually come from a man, a doctor a stand-up comedian all rolled into one, Dr Russell Kennedy, and they came from his bestselling book *Anxiety RX*. I don't want to blow his trumpet too much but feel I must.. If anyone is struggling with anxiety, trauma, any kind of childhood trauma, you need to think about investing in this book. It really is a must have in unravelling your thought process and giving you validation.

I scrutinised, read , reread and highlighted everything that was me. Because we're told where we should be, where we're expected to be and what we should be doing, but if your body is telling you something totally different, what are you supposed to do! You just have to feel it, ride the wave, allow it to happen; in fact, that's what I had already been doing all my life, just trying to manage it in the best way I could, the only way I knew how to. I was only trying to protect myself. The reason things had escalated and life had become so unbearable was just because my body was telling my mind that it was time, it was ready to start processing and unravelling a lifetime of hurt. I'm not in any way trying to say that if you read this you'll be cured overnight, but it most definitely gives you an insight and understanding and hopefully the tools you'll need moving forward, even if it's just one more tool to add to that box.

Oh, I almost forgot just one more thing… Be kind to yourself.

27

Chapter 13

Do you know what you've done?

If I had the opportunity, that's the only question that I'd ask: "Do you know what you've done?" From that little girl you taught me how to lie, how to stay quiet, not have the ability to feel I could speak up. My family was most definitely complicit in this too, wanting to keep it hushed up. In life never feeling confident enough that I could speak up or confront a situation that was just totally wrong. I find myself now occasionally wearing my Big girl pants, I've had to distance myself from my family because there was so much damage being done and , when people are doing wrong, their doing wrong and it shouldn't be enabled or overlooked just because their family People need to take responsibility for themselves and their behaviour. Double standards always seem to be at play ; one rule for one and one for another.

Not being able to live a life, not being able to maintain friendships, struggling through school, my personal relationships allowing people to walk over me; while they were looking at my faults I was too busy overlooking theirs! Never having any confidence, thinking there is no point trying because I know I just won't be good enough.

The hardest thing that breaks my heart is how my mess has effected my son. He's missed out on so much, never gaining the proper skills to feel comfortable in social situations, never having a normal childhood, going to the park or being able to have hardly any experiences, all because of me being afraid to go out, and for that I can never forgive myself.

I don't think abusers would be capable of understanding the damage they have caused. Do people ever really think about the consequences of certain actions and how you have single-handedly altered the course of someone's life and how it maybe could've been? I just hope whether he's watching from up above or down below, he's been made to see the destruction he caused.

Chapter 14

No-one knows

No-one knows or will ever know and understand unless they've gone through sexual abuse, and as much as I was desperate to talk to someone and for them to help me, in one way I'm glad they couldn't because they hadn't encountered it themselves, and that's something I wouldn't wish on anybody. Nobody can ever understand the weirdness of your actions or thoughts, those thoughts that swirl dominantly in your head at 2 a.m. when you can't sleep. I think that's why it's hard to maintain any kind of relationship, because you're on a different wave length, going out. Eating out , the cinema or even grocery shopping is just a no because you're in constant survival mode and it physically and mentally wears you down and totally exhausts you.

I don't care what anyone says or tells you to do: unless you're ready in yourself and at a stage where you can work through it, it's just going to be a waste of time. It's baby steps and by no way is it going to be an easy task, or a fast one! One thing I always felt were what people thought when they see you being emotional at the drop of a hat and not being able to always control it and them thinking, *Gosh, she's just a complete mess. She can't even control her emotions!* But let those tears fall because you need that release. If anything, it's a good thing; it just shows that we're human. I'd be more worried if I was unable to show any emotion; and just remember, no-one else walks in your shoes, so they haven't got a right to comment on how you walk in them! In actual fact, while they're thinking you're weak and you can't handle certain things, I wonder how many of them would be able to cope with that extra backpack you carry on your shoulders each day before you even start with just everyday bullxxxx. So you're actually stronger than you think, more than you allow yourself credit for, because you're carrying that extra burden, and look how long you've had to carry it around for. That's not weak, it's strength and you just continue to carry on even when you feel you can't. But you do.

We've missed out on so much and always been too cautious to live, constantly worrying what's coming in that next minute, that next hour. But try to take pleasure in those little things, because it's those little things that are the best, no matter how simple they may feel. We are very much alone. It's so hard trying to find people the same as us. Someone replied when I asked them, "Where are people like you and me?" She said, "We are there, its just hard to find us because we're all hiding." Well I wish they would all show themselves! All we can keep doing is our best, whatever that best may be. We all need to take a minute and think because we really don't know what someone else is having to deal with.

Afterthought

I'm still not understanding how this issue is still not being addressed or spoken about openly, because until these kinds of people are stopped, it's just going to carry on while we as a society keep on turning a blind eye, perhaps because of the nature of the problem, I think it's that shame or stigma around the whole sexual part of it. We need to be able to speak up where we can. Let's speak for those who can't; let's try easing their burden and let them know we stand by them.

Remember, when things were brought out into the open about "certain predators" in Hollywood in the celebrity world, which was a great step forward, it was because people who had the status and platform to do so did so, but what about the ordinary average person from a totally different environment where they don't have a platform or a voice as a child when a parent is sneaking into their room on an evening or where they're repeatedly taken to perhaps family, as childcare is needed and that whole situation is being taken fully advantage of, a parent unaware that it's not a safe place for their children? What about that? That child does not stand a chance. From that point on, that child's life is ruined, and they will go on – that's if they're even able to, to a life full of struggle and suffering, a never-ending battle with their self-worth. That's no way of life for anyone.

So who's standing up for those children? Who wants them to live a full life that they deserve to have, from no fault of their own? It's just snatched away from them. We need to be stepping up and looking out for one another. I certainly won't be shushed any longer. Will you?

I hope you find time to be happy and not just strong

X